leaf book

Planet Protectors

Look Out for Litter

Lisa Bullard

illustrated by Xiao Xin

M MILLBROOK PRESS · MINNEAPOLIS

For Donna G. —L.B.

Millbrook Press
A division of Lerner Publishing Group, Inc.
241 First Avenue North
Minneapolis, MN 55401 U.S.A.

Website address: www.lernerbooks.com

Main body text set in Slappy Inline 18/28.
Typeface provided by T26.

Library of Congress Cataloging-in-Publication Data

Bullard, Lisa.
    Look out for litter / by Lisa Bullard ; illustrated by Xiao Xin.
      p.   cm. — (Cloverleaf books™—Planet protectors)
    Includes index.
    ISBN 978-0-7613-6105-3 (lib. bdg. : alk. paper)
    1. Litter (Trash)—Juvenile literature. 2. Waste minimization—Juvenile
literature. I. Xiao Xin, ill. II. Title.
    TD813.B37 2012
    363.72'8—dc22   2010048869

Manufactured in the United States of America
1 – BP – 7/15/11

TABLE OF CONTENTS

Chapter One

Trina the Trash Stopper

Ahoy there! I'm Trina.

My pirate name is Trina the Trash Stopper.

But I'm not just a pirate.
I'm also an Earth saver. And **too much trash** is a big problem for our Earth.

Sometimes people throw their trash right on the ground. Or in the water. That's called **littering**.

Those people better watch out. Pirates don't like litter. They might toss litterers to the sharks!

Some people litter by accident. Ever lose a balloon? The balloon becomes litter when it lands. Ever try for a basket and miss the trash can? Try again, or that's litter too!

Yarr! I play pirate whenever we come to the beach.

But I'm not searching for treasure.
I'm searching for litter.

Every piece I pick up makes the **Earth cleaner.**

Be smart when you pick up litter. Ask a grown-up for help if you don't know what something is or if the litter looks sharp. Wear gloves or wash your hands afterward.

When I was little, I didn't understand how one piece of trash could be such a big deal.

But my dad explained that **litter causes huge problems.** It's worse than a hole in a pirate ship!

Litter leads to big messes. Litter on the road can lead to car crashes. People can cut themselves on broken glass. Litter can make our drinking water dirty.

Litter is really sneaky. It won't stay put. You might drop a plastic bag in your own yard.

But guess what? The wind can blow that bag somewhere else.

Plastic bags and paper bags are big litter problems. Find containers you can use over and over again. Bring your own cloth bags when your family goes shopping. Carry a lunch box instead of paper lunch bags.

Rain can wash litter from the ground into storm drains. From there, litter travels to **rivers and lakes.**

Lots of litter even reaches the oceans.
You better believe that makes us pirates mad!

Sometimes floating ocean trash gathers together in big areas. Look on a map of the United States. Can you find the state of Texas? One floating trash pile is about twice as big as Texas!

Litter in the water or on land **hurts animals.**

You know those plastic rings that hold together cans? Animals get them caught around their necks.

Whales and sea turtles sometimes try to eat plastic bags. The animals can get sick and die.

Always cut up plastic rings before throwing them away.

Chapter Three

Less Litter and Less Trash!

It's important to put litter in the trash can. But we need to **make less trash** too. The people who take away trash usually burn it or bury it.

Burning trash makes the air dirty. And even pirates can't find enough places to bury all of it.

What do you think, matey? Can you help me out with the litter problem?

Here are some easy ways to cut down on litter:
- Drink tap water instead of water from plastic bottles.
- Trade old toys with a friend instead of throwing them away.
- Don't buy things with lots of wrappers on them.
- Recycle everything you can.

By working together, we can fix it!

Then I can find a new way to
save the Earth tomorrow.

The "Looking for Litter" Game

There's so much litter around, some people hardly notice it. But once you begin to look, you see it almost everywhere. So start playing the "Looking for Litter" game. Your family can play it at the park or the beach. You can play it when you take your dog for a walk. Here's how to play:

What you need:

a small trash bag

a notebook

a pencil

any number of people

Write everybody's name in the notebook. Remind each person to look for litter. Put a mark next to the name each time someone picks some up. (Remember the safety rules on page 9.) At the end of each week, add up the marks. Who has picked up the most litter? The winner gets a prize!

Decide with your family what the prize should be. Maybe the winner gets to choose what kind of pizza to have. Or what game to play after dinner. Maybe he or she gets a nickel for every piece of litter. That's like finding a pirate's treasure!

Remember, there will be two winners each week. One winner is the person with the most marks. The other winner is the Earth!

GLOSSARY

burn: to set something on fire

bury: to dig a hole in the ground, put an object in the hole, and cover it with dirt

litter: trash that a person puts in the wrong place

plastic: something invented by people that can be made into things such as water bottles and toys

recycle: to turn trash into something that people can use

storm drain: an opening where water flows off a road or other flat area in a heavy rain

BOOKS

Bullard, Lisa. *Rally for Recycling.* Minneapolis: Millbrook Press, 2011. This book has more information on one of the best ways to fight litter: recycling.

Green, Jen. *Garbage and Litter.* New York: PowerKids Press, 2010. This book has more information about how people create litter and how you can keep Earth clean.

Hock, Peggy. *Our Earth: Keeping It Clean.* New York: Children's Press, 2009. Learn much more about pollution in this fact-filled book.

WEBSITES

Keep America Beautiful: Clean Sweep U.S.A.
http://www.cleansweepusa.org/default.aspx
Learn more at this website from Keep America Beautiful. You'll find comic books and lots more facts about litter and how you can prevent it.

NOAA: Understanding Marine Debris
http://marinedebris.noaa.gov/marinedebris101/ActivBk_pop.html
Visit this website from the National Oceanic and Atmospheric Administration to find a fun activity book. Learn more about ocean litter with the book's puzzles and coloring pages.

Texas Department of Transportation: Litter Force
http://www.dontmesswithtexas.org/litterforce
Check out this website from the Texas Department of Transportation. You'll find cool superhero games that will teach you more about litter.